I0812656

Wise Words of STEAM

100 TECHNOLOGY WORDS EXPLAINED

JON RICHARDS

Cavendish Square

Published in 2025 by Cavendish Square Publishing, LLC
2544 Clinton Street, Buffalo, NY 14224

First published in Great Britain in 2021 by Wayland

Series editor: John Hort
Designed and edited by Tall Tree Ltd

Picture Credits
FC-front cover, BC-back cover, t-top, b-bottom, l-left, r-right, c-center
1–48 Sandra_M/Shutterstock.com, 4c mountainpix/Shutterstock.com, 5b Rudiecast/Shutterstock.com, 6tr YAZZIK/Shutterstock.com, 6b Gorodenkoff/Shutterstock.com, 7tl MarinaGrigorivna/Shutterstock.com, 7b My Portfolio/Shutterstock.com, 10b giocalde/Shutterstock.com, 11b Radu Bercan/Shutterstock.com, 12c Dario Lo Presti/Shutterstock.com, 12br MPS Pro Group/Shutterstock.com, 13tr Oleksiy Mark/Shutterstock.com, 13c Pixel-Shot/Shutterstock.com, 13bl Jenson/Shutterstock.com, 14tr Maridav/Shutterstock.com, 14br Flegere/Shutterstock.com, 15t Sashkin/Shutterstock.com, 15bl Zyn Chakrapong/Shutterstock.com, 16tl ImageFlow/Shutterstock.com, 16b Roman Samborskyi/Shutterstock.com, 17t DenPhotos/Shutterstock.com, 17c 7heaven/Shutterstock.com, 17b Den Rozhnovsky/Shutterstock.com, 18t DGLimages/Shutterstock.com, 18c sixth/Shutterstock.com, 18b FREEPIK2/Shutterstock.com, 19t mkfilm/Shutterstock.com, 19b edel/Shutterstock.com, 20–21 Nikelser Kate/Shutterstock.com, 20t Nearbirds/Shutterstock.com, 20b Aratehortua/Shutterstock.com, 23t Wachiwit/Shutterstock.com, 23c UfaBizPhoto/Shutterstock.com, 23b BallBall14/Shutterstock.com, 24tr PanyaStudio/Shutterstock.com, 24b wavebreakmedia/Shutterstock.com, 25t itsmejust/Shutterstock.com, 25b and 29t i viewfinder/Shutterstock.com, 26c Ody_Stocker/Shutterstock.com, 26b schankz/Shutterstock.com, 27t Nataly Studio/Shutterstock.com, 27c Chaikom/Shutterstock.com, 27br SciePro/Shutterstock.com, 27bl Snailstudio/Shutterstock.com, 28t asharkyu/Shutterstock.com, 28b Gorodenkoff/Shutterstock.com, 29cr seyephoto/Shutterstock.com, 29b Gukzilla/Shutterstock.com, 30tr Dean Drobot/Shutterstock.com, 30b TLaoPhotography/Shutterstock.com, 31t Chromatika Multimedia snc/Shutterstock.com, 31b Marcin Kadziolka/Shutterstock.com, 32tl Matej Kastelic/Shutterstock.com, 32b Takashmi Images/Shutterstock.com, 33t jules2000/Shutterstock.com, 33c Hadrian/Shutterstock.com, 33b cy obo/Shutterstock.com, 34b Andrey Armyagov/Shutterstock.com, 35t Triff/Shutterstock.com, 35c Elenarts/Shutterstock.com, 35b Zenobillis/Shutterstock.com, 36c NicoElNino/Shutterstock.com, 37tr your/Shutterstock.com, 37tl Willyam Bradberry/Shutterstock.com, 37bl Rudmer Zwerver/Shutterstock.com, 37br Burben/Shutterstock.com, 38c beeboys/Shutterstock.com, 38b Maria Savenko/Shutterstock.com, 39tr pisotskii/Shutterstock.com, 39cl Oleksiy Mark/Shutterstock.com, 39br Tero Vesalainen/Shutterstock.com, 40b Anton Gvozdikov/Shutterstock.com, 41t Ankit K Sinha/Shutterstock.com, 41b MIKHAIL GRACHIKOV/Shutterstock.com, 42tl nexusby/Shutterstock.com, 42cl 26ShadesOFGreen/Shutterstock.com, 42br and 43t FrameStockFootages/Shutterstock.com, 43c elena09/Shutterstock.com, 43b Denis Simonov/Shutterstock.com, 44t Joe Gough/Shutterstock.com, 44b YEINISM/Shutterstock.com, 45t Martin M303/Shutterstock.com, 45c ESstock/Shutterstock.com, 45b Brent Hofacker/Shutterstock.com, 46tl gorosan/Shutterstock.com, 46c Natalia Ruedisueli/Shutterstock.com, 46b Creatikon Studio/Shutterstock.com, 47t Alena Ozerova/Shutterstock.com, 47b Kaspars Grinvalds/Shutterstock.com.

Cataloging-in-Publication Data

Names: Richards, Jon.
Title: 100 technology words explained / Jon Richards.
Description: Buffalo, New York : Cavendish Square Publishing, 2025. |
Series: Wise words of STEAM | Includes index.
Identifiers: ISBN 9781502671691 (pbk.) | ISBN 9781502671707 (library bound) |
ISBN 9781502671714 (ebook)
Subjects: LCSH: Technology--Terminology--Juvenile literature.
Classification: LCC T9.R53 2025 | DDC 603--dc23

CPSIA compliance information: Batch #CSCSQ25: For further information contact Cavendish Square Publishing LLC at 1-877-980-4450.

Printed in the United States of America

CONTENTS

AMAZING INVENTIONS

Throughout history, improvements in technology have allowed us to create machines that make our life easier, vehicles that can travel faster and more efficiently, and gadgets that let us relax and have fun.

1: Invention

Something that has never been made before.

FANTASTIC FACT

Some of the earliest inventions were simple tools, such as hand axes, which prehistoric human ancestors started to use about 10 million years ago.

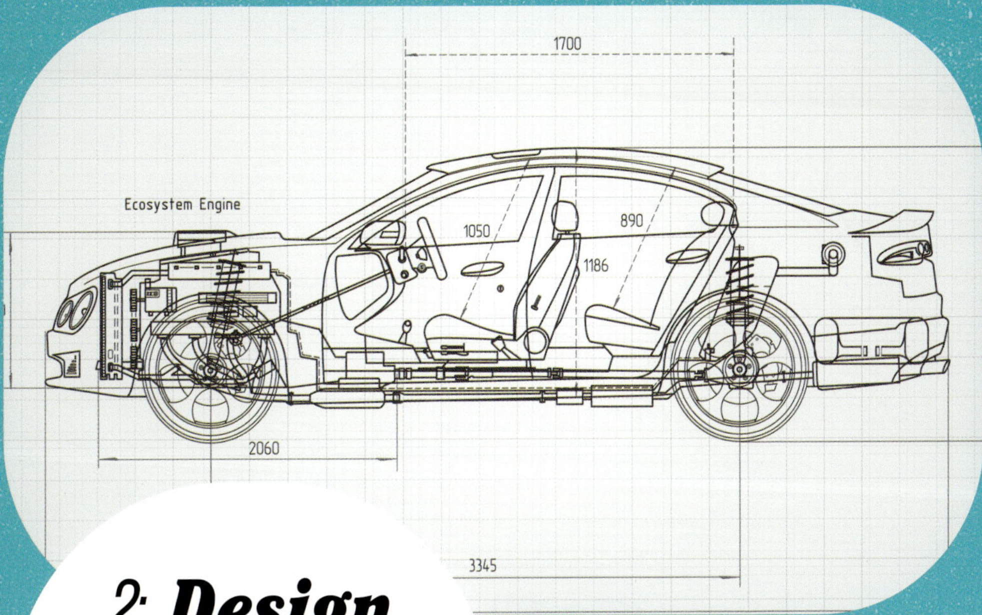

2: Design

To make a detailed plan or drawing of something. A design shows how to make and manufacture a device or material.

3: Prototype

The first example of a new object. Prototypes are used to check that a new device can be made and find out if it works as intended.

DESIGNING THINGS

Before anything can be made, a designer needs to create detailed plans and drawings to show how it could be put together, and to check how it would work.

4: *Plan drawing*

A plan or drawing that shows the shapes of individual parts and how they are put together.

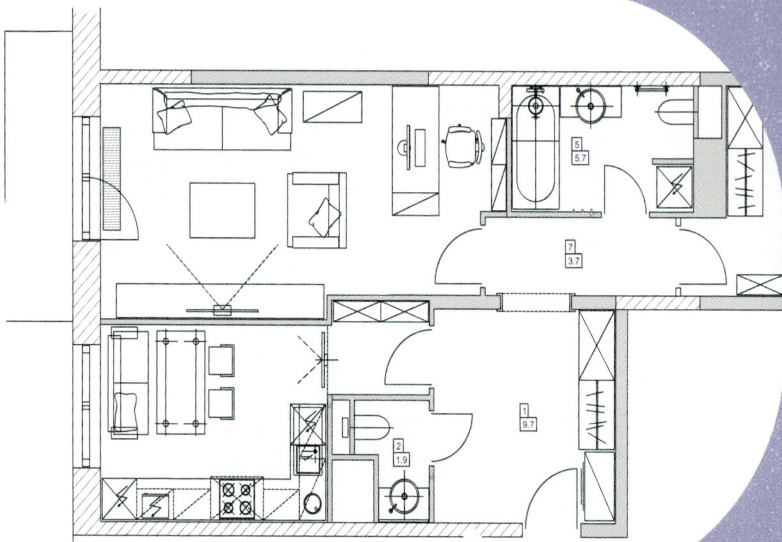

5: *CAD*

Short for "computer-aided design," this involves using a computer to help with the design of an object or machine, such as a car.

6: *3D printer*

A device that makes three-dimensional objects by adding many specially shaped thin layers of a material on top of each other. 3D printing lets designers make and test different models before they go into production.

FANTASTIC FACT

3D-printed objects can be made from a wide range of materials, such as plastics, metals, and even food!

7: *Nanotechnology*

Materials and devices made using particles that are so small that they can only be seen using a powerful microscope. For example, graphene is a nanotechnology material. It is made from a single sheet of carbon atoms and is very light and very strong, which gives designers the chance to create hard-wearing objects that are also flexible.

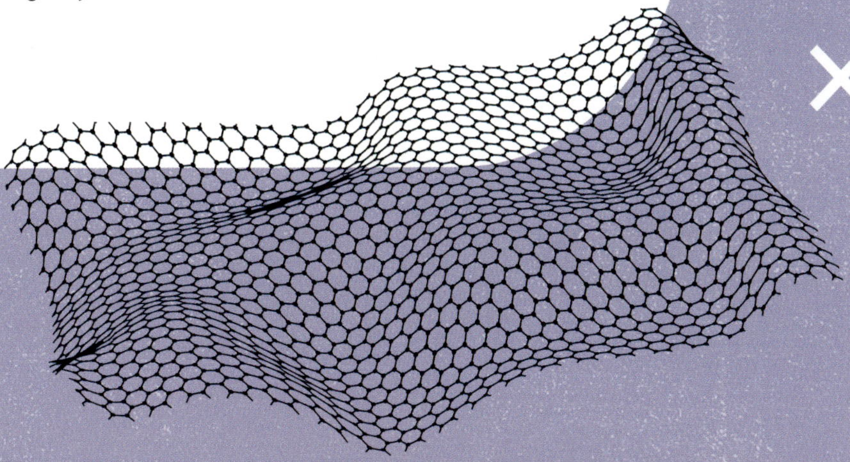

RESEARCH AND DEVELOPMENT

Part of the design stage is the testing of an object or material. Designs may be revised in response to these tests, and then the new design will be tested again—or the whole thing could be scrapped if it doesn't work at all!

8: ***Modeling***

To use a computer program or mathematical formulas to test something to see if it will work.

9: ***Testing***

To try out an object, substance, or idea in order to collect data (information) about it and see if it will work.

10: *Artificial intelligence*

Also known as AI, this is the ability of a computer to work in an intelligent way. The computer learns from what happens to it and what it does, rather than being given specific instructions. Designers can use AI applications to test objects and materials digitally before they make a prototype.

FANTASTIC FACT

AI technology is already being used to analyze huge amounts of medical data and to look at how air pollution could affect climate change.

PRINTING AND BOOKS

Modern books are produced in their millions using huge, super-fast printing machines. However, the earliest books had to be written and drawn by hand, which took a long time and was very expensive.

AaBbCcDdEeFf
GgHhIiJjKkLl
MmNnOoPpQq
RrSsTtUuVvWw
XxYyZz
0123456789

11: *Typeface*

A collection of letters, numbers, and symbols that have been designed to look similar to each other. Type is grouped into fonts, where all the letters, numbers, and symbols use similar shapes. The font on the left is ITC Cheltenham.

12: *Print*

To apply a pattern, drawing, or text to a material, such as paper or cloth. When large numbers of books or newspapers are printed, this is usually done by making metal plates with raised lines containing the type and illustrations. These plates are covered with ink and then pushed against sheets of paper. Customers can order individual books with print-on-demand (POD), which uses digital printing to produce one copy at a time.

FANTASTIC FACT

Before the creation of books as we know them, information was written down on lots of different materials, such as clay tablets, papyrus sheets, rolls of paper called scrolls, and even pieces of bone.

13: *Page*

One side of a sheet of paper in a book, magazine, or newspaper.

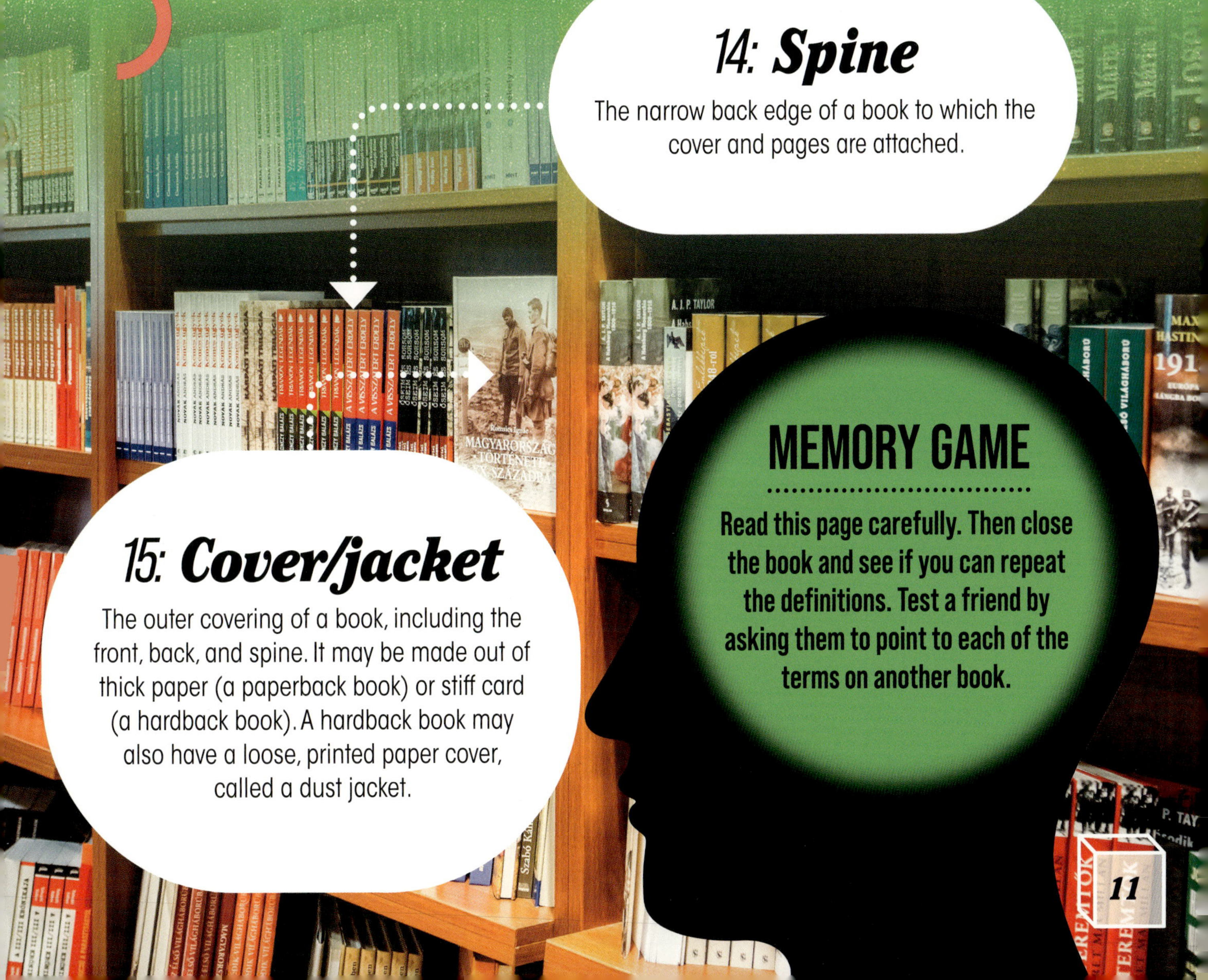

14: *Spine*

The narrow back edge of a book to which the cover and pages are attached.

15: *Cover/jacket*

The outer covering of a book, including the front, back, and spine. It may be made out of thick paper (a paperback book) or stiff card (a hardback book). A hardback book may also have a loose, printed paper cover, called a dust jacket.

MEMORY GAME

Read this page carefully. Then close the book and see if you can repeat the definitions. Test a friend by asking them to point to each of the terms on another book.

ELECTRONICS

Modern electronic devices use technology to carry out a large number of jobs in the blink of eye. This allows electronic gadgets to do these tasks over and over again without making a mistake.

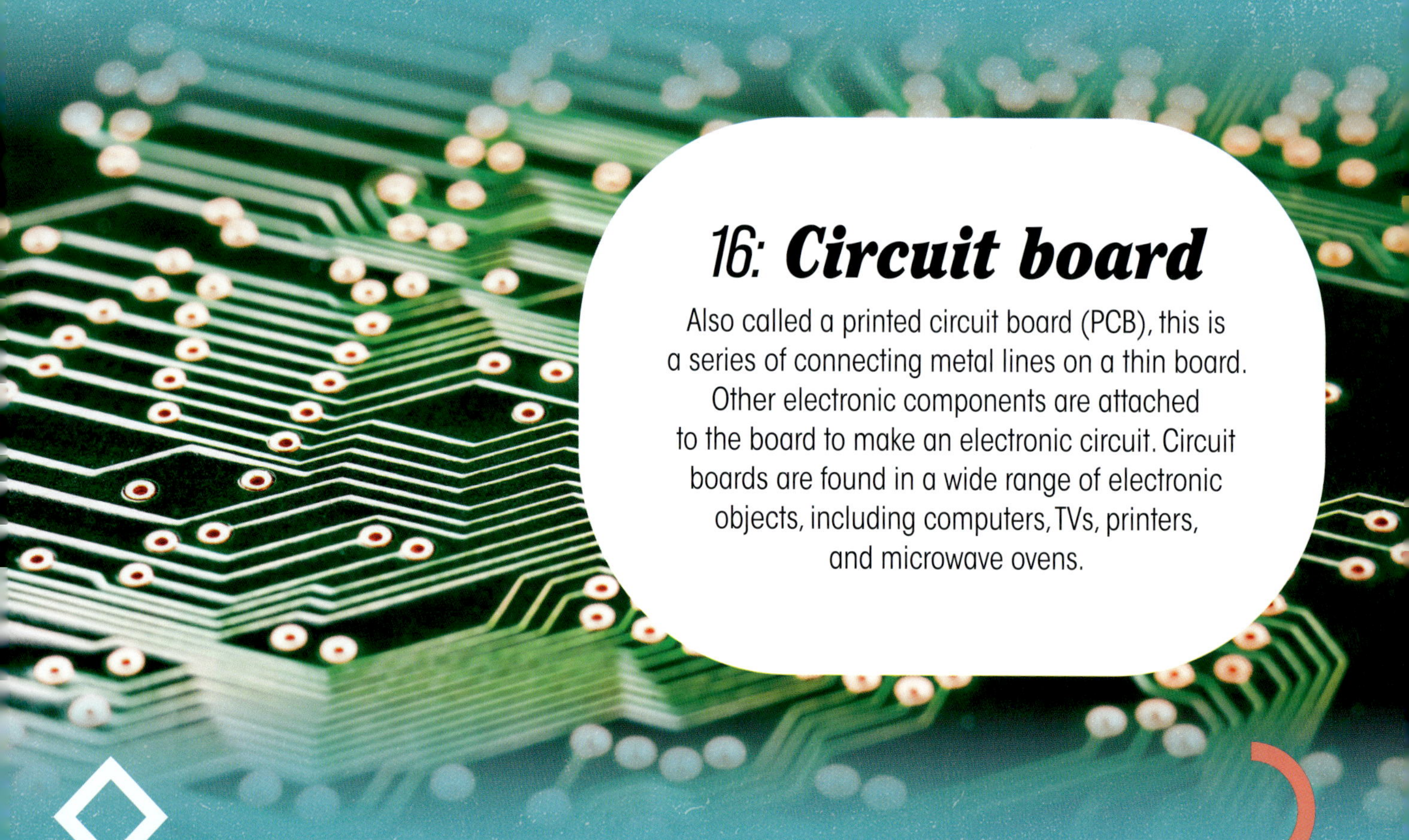

16: *Circuit board*

Also called a printed circuit board (PCB), this is a series of connecting metal lines on a thin board. Other electronic components are attached to the board to make an electronic circuit. Circuit boards are found in a wide range of electronic objects, including computers, TVs, printers, and microwave ovens.

17: *LED*

Short for "Light-Emitting Diode." A small device that glows when an electric current is passed through it.

18: **LCD**

Short for "liquid crystal display." A flat-screen device that uses special liquid crystals that become visible when electricity passes through them. Different parts of the display can be switched on or off by an electronic circuit to make text or patterns.

19: **Sensor**

A device that detects something, such as changes in light or movement.

20: **Actuator**

A part of a machine that moves another part. A robot arm has electric motors, which act as actuators to move parts of the arm.

COMMUNICATIONS

Today, we can send signals to the other side of the planet and beyond at the speed of light! This lets us see TV footage from distant countries, stream movies on a laptop, and even control robot rovers on distant worlds!

21: *Bluetooth*

A method that uses radio waves to allow electronic devices–such as computers, speakers, mobile phones, and headphones–to send information to each other over short distances without using wires.

FANTASTIC FACT

Bluetooth technology is named after a Scandinavian king from the 900s CE. Harald Gormsson ruled Denmark and Norway and had a noticeable dead tooth, which looked blue, so he had the nickname "Bluetooth." He is famous for uniting different parts of Scandinavia under his rule.

22: *Radio waves*

A form of electromagnetic radiation that can be used to send electrical signals over very long distances.

23: *Fiber optics*

Sending pulses of light along thin, transparent fibers to carry signals, such as internet data or TV programs.

24: *Microwaves*

A form of electromagnetic radiation that can be used to send signals, usually over short distances, or over longer distances in a system of relays (one station after the other). Microwaves can also be used to cook food by heating up the water inside it.

MEMORY GAME

Find objects around your home that use the technology mentioned on these pages. Can you remember which type of technology they use without looking at this book?

COMPUTING

You can find computer technology in a huge range of gadgets around the home, in schools, and in workplaces. It can control what you watch on TV, how you wash your clothes, and even help you to keep your refrigerator well-stocked with food.

25: *Processor*

The part of a computer that receives commands and follows a computer program to carry out certain tasks.

26: *Computer programmer*

A person who writes computer programs (a set of instructions for the computer to follow to complete a particular task) and inputs instructions into a computer.

27: *Software*

Another name for computer programs.

28: *Hardware*

The name given to the devices, such as computers, that are controlled by computer programs.

29: *RAM*

Short for "random-access memory," this is the part of a computer where information is temporarily stored while the computer is using it. A part called "read-only memory (ROM)" is where computer programs are stored permanently.

30: *Monitor*

A screen that displays the jobs a computer is carrying out.

THE INTERNET

Today, the Internet connects billions of "smart" objects around the planet, from computers and phones to kitchen gadgets, watches, cars, and even the clothes we wear.

31: *Internet*

The global computer network that allows people to access information on web pages and to send messages to each other using email.

32: *Modem*

A device that connects a computer to the Internet.

33: *Wi-Fi*

A method that lets a computer or other digital device connect to the Internet without using wires.

34: *Server*

A computer that stores information and can be accessed by other computers and smart devices.

FANTASTIC FACT

The first web page was set up in 1991. Thirty years later, there are nearly 1.75 billion (1,750,000,000) websites on the Internet.

35: *Network*

A system of connected devices, including servers, computers and other smart devices.

CODING

While computers and gadgets can do clever things, they still need to be given instructions to tell them what to do.

36: *Computer code*

The set of instructions that make up a computer program, telling a computer what jobs to carry out. There are many different "languages" used to create computer code.

```
<head>
        <title> Title of web page</title>
</head>
<body>
        <h1> This is the main heading
        <p> This is a paragraph of body text. </p>
```

Example: Title of web page

Link to actual web page

37: *Algorithm*

A set of instructions that tell something to perform a specific job. These step-by-step instructions are at the heart of all computer programs. In everyday life, a cooking recipe is a form of algorithm.

38: **Bug**

An error, usually a mistake in the computer code, that stops a computer program from running correctly.

OK

STOP! Critical error

39: **Computer virus**

A harmful piece of computer code that can copy itself, damaging any computer or smart device that it is put into.

OK

FANTASTIC FACT

The first computer virus was called "Brain." It was developed in 1986 and was actually meant to stop people from making pirate (illegal) copies of legal software.

GAMING

Modern video games combine computer hardware with super-sharp graphics, animation, and exciting plots to give you and your friends hours of fun and excitement.

40: *Computer graphics*

The pictures and animations used in computer images and games.

41: *Avatar*

An image that a person uses to represent themselves. Avatars can look like a person, simple graphics, or even a fantastical creature.

MEMORY GAME

Copy these definitions on flash cards and use them to test yourself, your friends, and your classmates.

42: Augmented reality

Combining the real world with computer-generated sounds, images, and text to add information or entertainment to real-life experiences. Augmented reality is used in various ways, including gaming, industrial design, and shopping.

43: Virtual reality

A computer simulation that recreates a real place or a completely imaginary one. Users often wear special headsets to allow them to look around the virtual world. Scientists can use virtual reality to test out machines before they are built, while gamers can explore and play in virtual worlds as part of a video game.

44: Gaming console

A device that has been specifically built to play video games. It usually includes special buttons on a controller or a joystick.

MEDICINE

The human body has the amazing ability to heal wounds, fight off diseases, and prevent itself from becoming ill. But every now and then, it needs an extra bit of technological help.

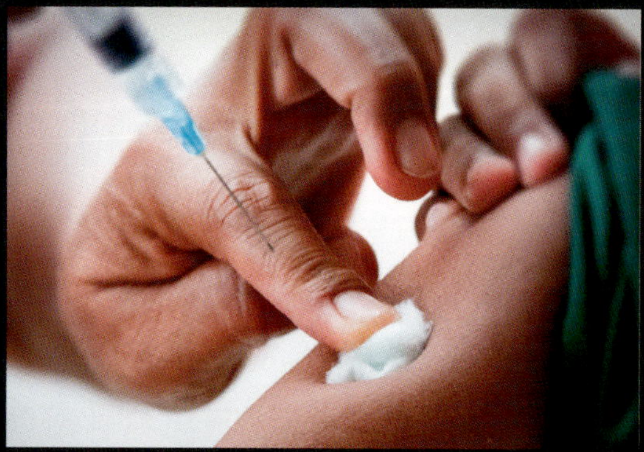

45: *Vaccination*

A medicine that helps to prevent an infection by a specific disease. Some vaccinations involve giving a weakened form of the disease they are designed to protect against. That way the body will be able to recognize the main disease if it becomes infected with it in the future and be able to attack it right away.

46: *Body scanner*

A machine that is used to see inside the body without having to cut the body open. Scanners use different forms of energy to "look" inside the body, including ultrasound (pictured below).

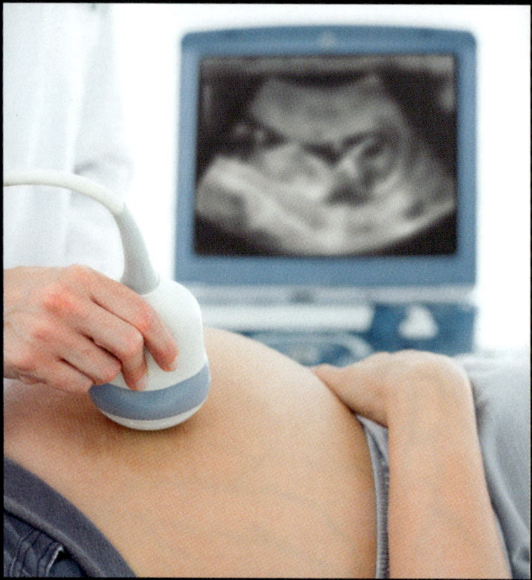

FANTASTIC FACT

The disease smallpox has been eradicated in the outside world thanks to a global vaccination program. It now only exists in a handful of laboratories where it is studied for research.

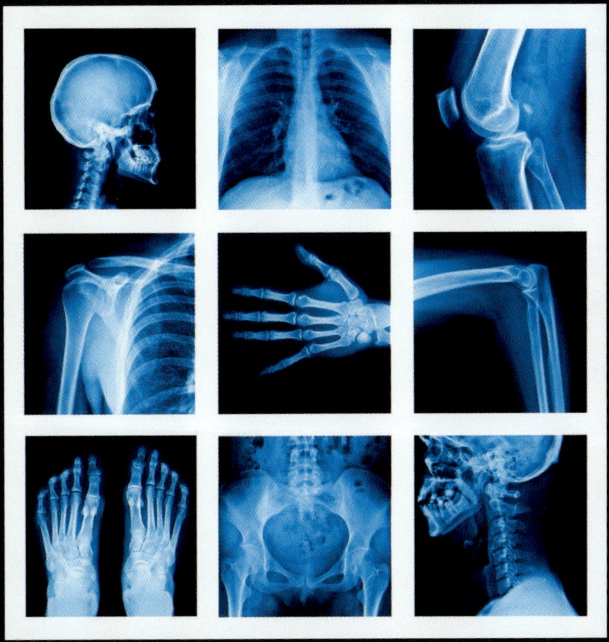

47: X-rays

A form of electromagnetic radiation that can pass through soft parts of your body, such as skin and muscles, but not hard parts, such as bones. X-ray images allow doctors to study the bones inside your body, and also soft parts that have been injected with special chemicals that block X-rays.

48: Antibiotics

A medicine that kills or stops the growth of tiny organisms, called bacteria. Antibiotics do not work against viruses, such as the ones that cause the common cold or flu (influenza).

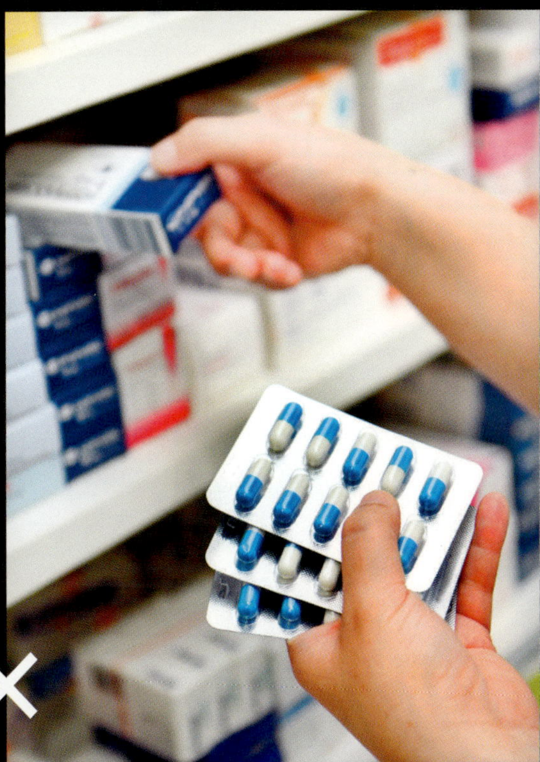

BIOTECHNOLOGY

Biotechnology involves using science and technology to change how a living thing looks, grows, and even behaves. Biotechnology uses living organisms, or parts of them, to develop new products. This can range from breeding new types of crop or animal to making medicines.

49: *DNA*

Short for deoxyribonucleic acid. This is a very long molecule that is arranged in a twisted spiral, called a double helix. It is found inside cells and it carries the genetic information (a set of coded instructions) that tells the cells how to look and behave.

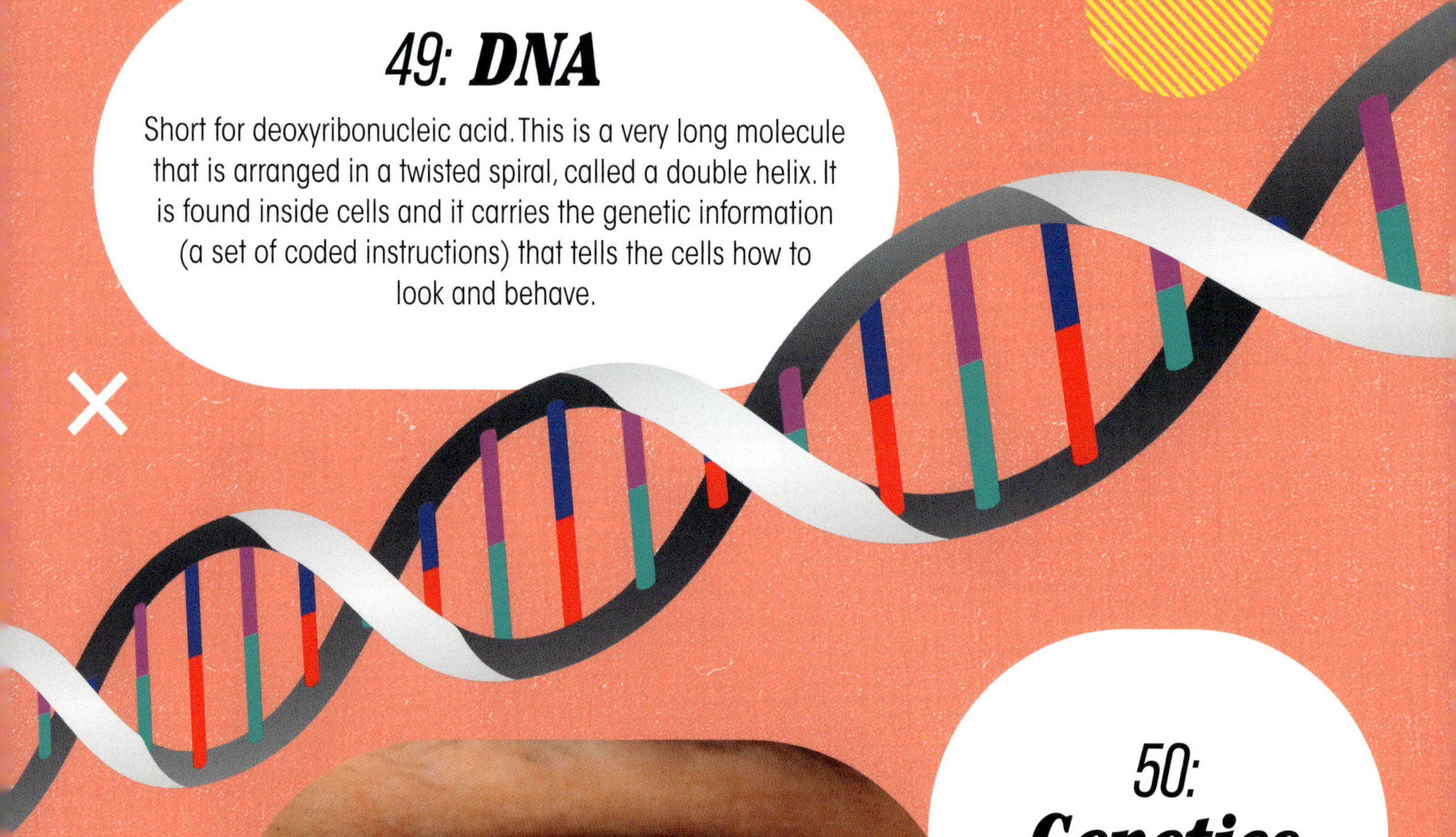

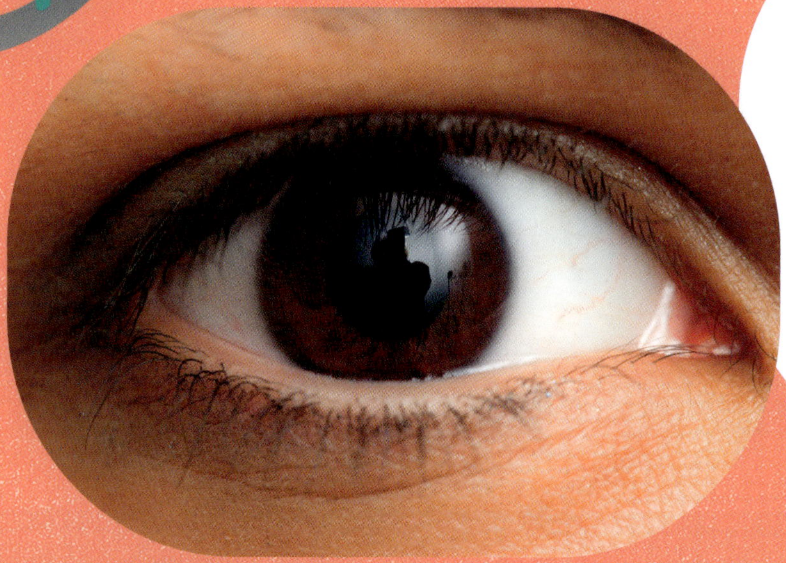

50: *Genetics*

The science of how living things inherit features from parents, and how DNA controls the body.

51: Genetically modified

A living thing whose DNA has been changed to make a feature better or to remove something that is undesirable. For example, bananas can be genetically modified to make them more resistant to disease.

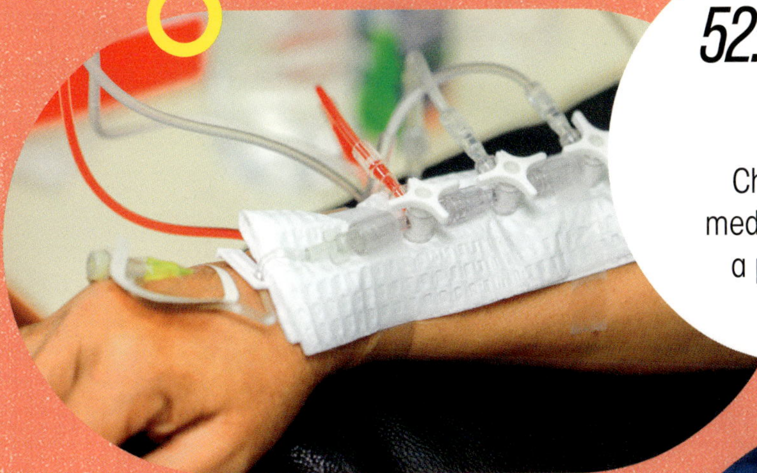

52: Drug delivery systems

Chemicals or devices that make sure a medicine reaches a specific target, such as a particular organ or tissue in the body.

53: Immunology

The science of how the human immune system protects the body from infection.

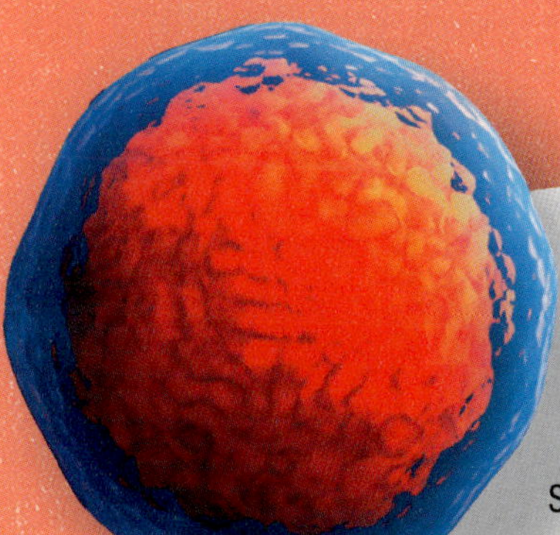

54: Stem cell

A type of cell that can duplicate and form other different specialist cells, such as white blood cells or nerve cells. Most cells in the body can only produce more cells like themselves.

FACTORY ENGINEERING

Around the world, huge factories churn out millions of products every day.

55: *Robot*

A machine that carries out jobs automatically in response to commands or computer programs.

56: *Production line*

A line of machines and people that each carry out a specific task to produce a finished object.

57: Automated

To carry out a job without having to receive instructions from humans. Robots are automated machines.

58: Manufacturing

Making objects and materials, usually on a large scale.

59: Quality control

A system to check that things are being made properly to do the job they are intended for.

SPORTS

With nail-biting action taking place in the blink of an eye, modern sports need the very latest in technological innovations to help athletes improve performance, and to help umpires or referees make fair decisions.

60: Artificial limb

An artificial body part that is designed to look and behave like a missing limb, such as an arm or leg. Athletes with artificial limbs are able to compete in sports events such as the Paralympic Games.

FANTASTIC FACT

Scientists have developed a composite material using graphene (see page 7) that is 10 times stronger than steel but extremely lightweight.

61: Composite materials

Materials that are made from two or more substances. Carbon fiber is a composite material made from thin strands of carbon that have been set in a resin. It is used to make parts of vehicles and machines that are lighter and stronger than metal parts would be, as well as sports equipment such as skis and tennis rackets.

62: *Hawk-Eye*

A method of plotting the path of a ball so that people can confirm where it went or even predict where it will go. In tennis, Hawk-Eye is used to check if a ball bounced inside or outside the court.

63: *VAR*

Short for video assistant referee, this is a system of cameras that a soccer referee can refer to and check if an offense has taken place, such as an attacking player being offside.

TRANSPORT

In the search for faster, more efficient, and safer ways to travel, engineers are developing new sources of power, and vehicles that can drive, sail, and even fly themselves!

64: *Hybrid car*

A type of car that uses electric motors alongside a traditional internal combustion (gas or diesel) engine.

65: *Hydrogen fuel cell*

A power source that combines hydrogen and oxygen to produce electricity, heat, and water. Fuel cells are small enough to be used in cars.

66: Drone

A ship or aircraft that has no crew and is controlled automatically by a computer, or by a person using radio controls from a distance.

67: LIDAR

A device that uses an infrared laser (a form of electromagnetic radiation) to judge the distance to other objects. Self-driving cars (vehicles driven by computers) use lidar systems to detect other cars and the side of the road. It works by sending out laser light and detecting its reflection from surrounding objects.

68: Maglev

Short for "magnetic levitation," this is a system of electromagnets that push against each other, causing a train to float above its track.

FANTASTIC FACT

Because a maglev train floats above the track, there is very little friction, allowing it to travel very fast. The fastest can travel at more than 372 miles (600 km) per hour.

SPACE TECHNOLOGY

Exploring the universe beyond Earth's atmosphere requires technology that can survive extreme conditions and still take measurements and make images. This information helps scientists to discover more about the stars and planets.

69: *Satellite*

An object that orbits (goes around) a planet. While natural satellites are known as moons (including our moon), artificial satellites are launched into orbit by rockets and are used to study planets and stars, study Earth's surface, or bounce signals and messages around the planet.

70: *Solar panel*

A part of a spacecraft that uses light from the sun to produce electricity. Solar panels are also used on Earth as a source of renewable electricity.

71: Rover

A space vehicle that is designed to drive over the surface of a moon or planet.

FANTASTIC FACT

The lunar rovers on the Apollo moon missions were driven by astronauts, while the different Mars rovers were designed to drive themselves or were operated remotely by people based back on Earth.

72: Space probe

A robot spacecraft that is designed to explore and study objects beyond Earth.

73: Spacesuit

A suit that is designed to keep an astronaut alive in the cold vacuum of space while they are outside their spacecraft.

FINDING YOUR WAY

With the help of modern technology, you need never get lost again, whether you're up a mountain, deep underwater, or even thousands of feet (m) in the air.

74: GPS

Short for "global positioning system." This is a network of satellites around Earth that are used to pinpoint someone's position on the planet.

FANTASTIC FACT

GPS systems are so accurate that, with the right equipment, they can tell your position to within a few inches (cm).

75: Sonar

A system that detects objects underwater using sound waves.

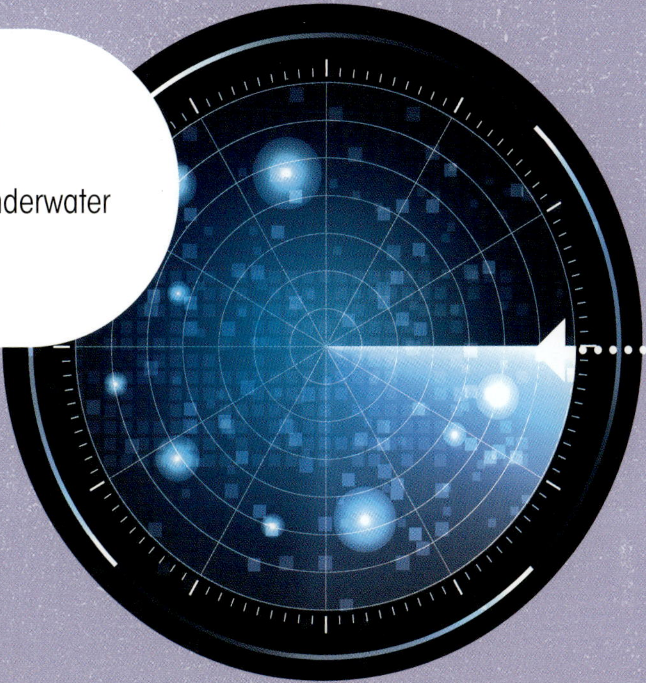

FANTASTIC FACT

Dolphins and bats use a form of sonar to detect objects and prey.

Sonar and radar collect sound or radio signals that bounce off objects. They then use these "echoes" to calculate where the objects are and even how fast they are moving.

76: Radar

A system that detects objects by bouncing radio waves off them.

HOME ENTERTAINMENT

From the comfort of your couch you can access a wide range of entertainment technology that can supply you with music, movies, and live events from around the globe at the click of a button.

77: *Smart speaker*

A loudspeaker that can answer spoken commands and is connected to the Internet. Smart speakers can give you lots of information, such as the latest sports results and weather reports, and even play music for you on request.

78: *Smartphone*

A mobile phone that can operate apps (applications, or computer programs), connect to the Internet and send e-mails, as well as make phone calls.

79: Surround sound

A system of speakers arranged around a room to give the impression that you are surrounded with sound while watching a film or TV program.

80: HDTV

Short for "high-definition television." This is a type of television that can produce very sharp and clear pictures.

81: Stream

To play films, TV programs, and music directly from the Internet without having to download them.

PRODUCING AND STORING ELECTRICITY

Modern technology needs safe, cheap, and environmentally friendly sources of power.

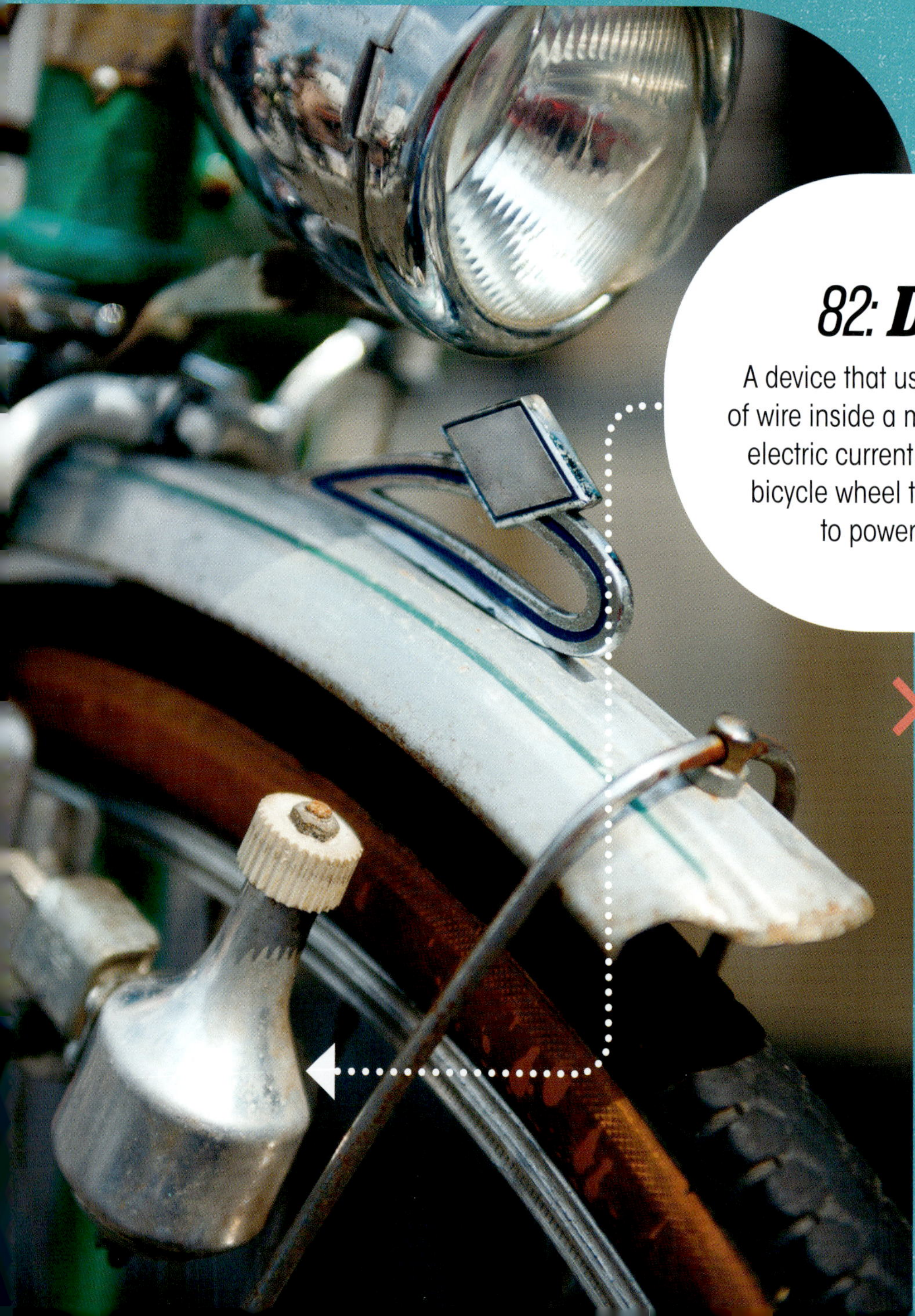

82: *Dynamo*

A device that uses the movement of a coil of wire inside a magnetic field to produce an electric current. This dynamo spins as the bicycle wheel turns. It provides electricity to power the bicycle's lights.

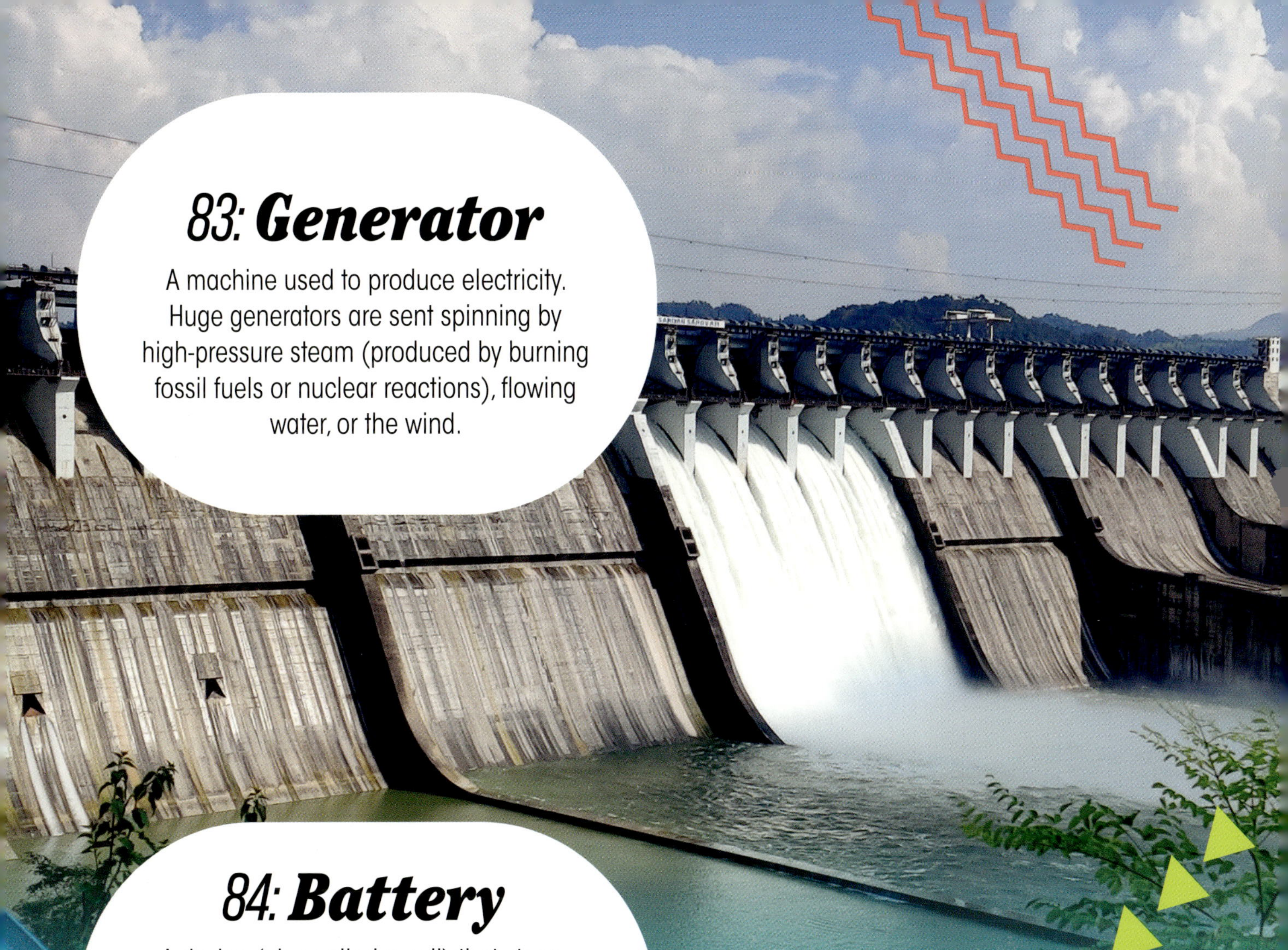

83: Generator

A machine used to produce electricity. Huge generators are sent spinning by high-pressure steam (produced by burning fossil fuels or nuclear reactions), flowing water, or the wind.

84: Battery

A device (also called a cell) that stores electricity. A battery converts stored chemical energy into electricity when it is connected to a complete electrical circuit.

FANTASTIC FACT

The city of Adelaide, Australia, has a huge battery installation that, when it was built in 2017, could store 129 megawatt-hours of electricity produced by nearby wind turbines – enough to power 30,000 homes for eight hours.

FILM AND TV

Lights, camera, action! These technology innovations will make your trip to the movie theater (or an evening in your living room) as exciting and entertaining as possible.

85: *Aspect ratio*

The ratio between the width and height of a TV or cinema screen. Many TVs have an aspect ratio of 16:9, which is widescreen.

86: *Cinematography*

The art and craft of making motion pictures, including the skills needed to operate the lights and cameras.

87: *Editing suite*

The room where sequences of film are cut and put together to make the finished film or program.

88: Recording studio

The room where sound effects are created after a film or TV show has been filmed. Everyday objects are often used to mimic sounds, such as a pair of gloves for flapping bird wings or large thin metal plates that are shaken to recreate thunder.

89: Digital technology

Using electronic devices to record and store information, such as images and sounds. Early films were recorded onto reels of celluloid film, while modern movies are recorded onto digital hard drives.

90: CGI

Short for "computer-generated imagery." These are special effects and even whole images that are created using computer graphics rather than photographing real-life objects.

FOOD TECHNOLOGY

The food you put into your body is a result of thousands of years of development as well as modern technological improvements designed to make what you eat last longer and taste better.

91: *Additives*

Substances that are added to food to improve flavors or to keep food fresh for longer.

92: *Vertical farming*

Growing crops in vertical racks. Plants are grown using special chemicals rather than soil and under artificial lights rather than sunlight.

93: Fermenting

Using microorganisms, such as yeast or bacteria, to break down material from plants to make other substances. Brewing beer and making wine both involve fermentation.

94: Roasting

To cook something using hot air from an open fire or inside an oven.

95: Dehydrated

Something that has had all the water removed from it. Dehydrating a food will make it last for a very long time.

TEXTILES

Developments in garment and material technology mean that the clothes you wear will fit you well and keep you warm or cool – they may even be able to work out if you're feeling unwell.

96: Weaving

To make a fabric by interlacing vertical and horizontal threads. Some threads are held stationary in the loom (warp threads), and the remaining threads (weft threads) are woven under and over the warp ones.

97: Knitting

To make a fabric by looping together single or multiple different threads. Knitted materials are often stretchy (unlike woven fabrics).

98: Smart materials

These are materials that can change in response to different situations. Some smart materials will change their color when temperatures change or when they get wet, while others can repair themselves if they become damaged.

99: Artificial fibers

These are fibers that have been made by a chemical process, rather than made from natural sources such as wool or cotton. Nylon and acrylic are types of artificial fibers.

100: Wearable technology

Devices that can be part of a garment or worn as accessories, such as rings, bracelets ,or watches. Wearable technology can record lots of information about you and your body, such as the number of steps you take each day, or how quickly your heart is beating.

INDEX